The Bridge

by
Linda Edwards Beal

Published by Piscataqua Press
142 Fleet St. Portsmouth, NH 03801
www.ppressbooks.com
info@piscataquapress.com

Printed in the United States of America

All proceeds from this book will benefit the Portsmouth School Department

Here is the bridge.

The cars can go across

the bridge.

The bus can go across

the bridge.

The truck can go across

the bridge.

The people can go across

the bridge.

The dog can go across

the bridge.

Here is the bridge.

The bird can go over

the bridge.

The bird can go under

the bridge.

The birds can go on the bridge.

Here is the bridge.

The bridge can go up,

and up,

and up!

The boat can go under

the bridge.

Look at the bridge.

MEMORIAL TO THE SAILORS AND SOLDIERS OF
NEW HAMPSHIRE
WHO PARTICIPATED IN THE WORLD WAR 1917-1919

1923   2013

The **Memorial Bridge** rests between Portsmouth, New Hampshire and Kittery, Maine. It was originally built in 1923 and then replaced in 2013.

The Memorial Bridge is a vertical-lift bridge. This means the center deck can rise up, staying parallel with the rest of the bridge, so boats can travel under. The counterweights and chains in the two towers weigh the same as the deck. The weights move down slowly as the center deck rises.

In the summer months, the bridge lifts every half hour so larger boats can travel under. It takes only a few minutes for the bridge to lift up, but it can be up to fifteen minutes before boat traffic clears and the deck returns back down. People often stop to watch the bridge go up.

The World War 1 Memorial Bridge was built in memory of the New Hampshire sailors and soldiers from 1917-1919. A plaque on the bridge reminds people of their bravery.